MW00907464

Angels

Ever in our Midst

A Special Gift

To

_____

From

_____

Date

_____

Little Ribbons of Love

Afternoon Tea: Taking Time for Friends

Angels: Ever in Our Midst

Flowers for a Friend

Sisters: So Much We Share

Angels

Ever in our Midst

Brownlow

Brownlow Publishing Company, Inc.

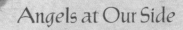

Angels at Our Side

"From glory unto glory,"

without a shade of care,

Because the Lord who loves us

will every burden bear;

Because we trust Him fully,
  and know that He will guide,
And know that blessed angels are
  watching at our side.

FRANCIS R. HAVERGAL

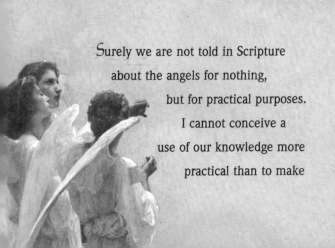

Surely we are not told in Scripture
about the angels for nothing,
but for practical purposes.
I cannot conceive a
use of our knowledge more
practical than to make

it connect the sight of this
world with the thought of another.
It is a great comfort to reflect that,
wherever we go, we have those about us,
who are ministering to all the heirs of
salvation, though we see them not.

S.J.C.

Peace

We shall find peace.

We shall hear the angels,

We shall see the sky

  sparkling with diamonds.

CHEKOV

Song of Praise

For the blessings of this day,
   For the mercies of this hour,
For the Bible's cheering ray,
   For the angel's protecting power,
Grateful notes to Thee we raise;
   Oh! accept our song of praise.

Nineteenth-Century Benediction

To wish to act
like angels while we
are still in this world
is nothing but folly.

TERESA OF AVILA

It was pride that changed
angels into devils;
it is humility that makes
men as angels.

AUGUSTINE

Angel Love

Unless you can love,
  as the angels may,
With the breadth of heaven
  betwixt you;
Unless you can dream
  that his faith is fast,

Through behoving
and unbehoving;
Unless you can die
when the dream is past,
Oh, never call it loving!

ROBERT BROWNING

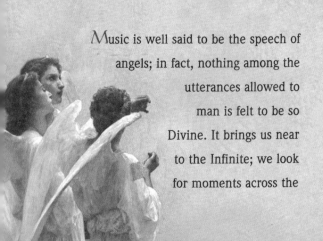

Music is well said to be the speech of angels; in fact, nothing among the utterances allowed to man is felt to be so Divine. It brings us near to the Infinite; we look for moments across the

cloudy elements into the eternal light,
when song leads and inspires us.
Serious nations, all nations that can
listen to the mandate of nature, have
prized song and music as a vehicle
for worship, for prophecy, and for
whatsoever in them was Divine.

THOMAS CARLYLE

How sweetly did they float
upon the wings
Of silence through the
empty-vaulted night,
At every fall smoothing
the raven down
Of darkness till it smiled!

JOHN MILTON

Angel Instincts

Not learned, save in gracious
  household ways,
Not perfect, nay, but full of
  tender wants,
No angel, but a dearer being,
  all dipt
In Angel instincts,
  breathing Paradise.

ALFRED, LORD TENNYSON

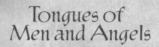

Tongues of
Men and Angels

If I speak in the tongues of men
and of angels, but have not love,
I am only a resounding gong or a
clanging cymbal. If I have the gift
of prophecy and can fathom all
mysteries and all knowledge,

and if I have a faith that can move mountains, but have not love, I am nothing. If I give all I possess to the poor and surrender my body to the flames, but have not love, I gain nothing.

1 Corinthians 13:1-3

Hidden Wings

How shall we tell an angel
   From another guest?
How, from the common worldly herd,
   One of the blest?
Hint of suppressed halo,
   Rustle of hidden wings,

Wafture of heavenly frankincense,—

Which is these things?

The old Sphinx smiles so subtly:

"I give no golden rule,—

Yet I would warn thee, World: treat well

Whom thou call'st fool."

GERTRUDE HALL

Unbless'd thy hand,
if, in this low disguise,
Wanders, perhaps,
some inmate of the skies.

HOMER

Good night,

sweet prince,

And flights of angels sing

thee to thy rest!

WILLIAM SHAKESPEARE

Angels are spirits, but it is not because they are spirits that they are angels. They become angels when they are sent. For the name *angel* refers to their office, not their nature. You ask the name of this nature, it is *spirit*; you ask its office, it is that of an angel, which is a messenger.

AUGUSTINE

Angel Lullabies

Out yonder in the moonlight,
   wherein God's Acre lies,
Go angels walking to and fro,
   singing their lullabies.
Their radiant wings are folded,
   and their eyes are bended low,
As they sing among the beds whereon
   the flowers delight to grow.

EUGENE FIELD

How fading are the joys we dote upon!

Like apparitions seen and gone.

But those which soonest take their flight

Are the most exquisite and strong—

Like angels' visits, short and bright;

Mortality's too weak to bear them long.

JOHN NORRIS

Earth Angels

But chiefly ye should lift your gaze
Above the world's uncertain haze,
And look with calm unwavering eye
On the bright fields beyond the sky,
Ye, who your Lord's commission bear,
His way of mercy to prepare:
Angels He calls ye: be your strife
To lead on earth an angel's life.

Think not of rest; though dreams
  be sweet,
Start up, and ply your heavenward feet.
Is not God's oath upon your head,
Ne'er to sink back on slothful bed,
Never again your loins untie,
Nor let your torches waste or die,

Till when the shadows
thickest fall,
Ye hear your Master's
midnight call?

JOHN KEBLE

In these days
you must go to Heaven
to find an angel.

POLISH PROVERB

When angels come,

the devils leave.

PROVERB

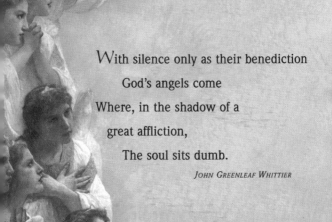

With silence only as their benediction

God's angels come

Where, in the shadow of a

great affliction,

The soul sits dumb.

JOHN GREENLEAF WHITTIER

The Angel that presided o'er my birth
Said, "Little creature, formed of joy
   and mirth,
Go love without the help of any thing
   on earth."

WILLIAM BLAKE

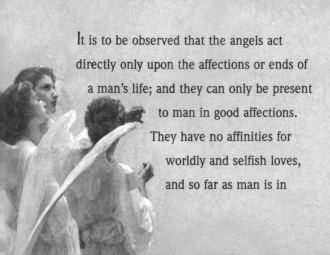

It is to be observed that the angels act
directly only upon the affections or ends of
a man's life; and they can only be present
to man in good affections.
They have no affinities for
worldly and selfish loves,
and so far as man is in

those loves, he removes himself from their protection and guidance. The angels are then more remote. They do all they can for him. But the amount of influence they can exert upon man depends upon what there is in man to receive it, to be acted upon. They come as near to every one as they can get.

CHAUNCEY GILES

See, I am sending an angel ahead of you to guard you along the way and to bring you to the place I have prepared. Pay attention to him and listen to what he says.

EXODUS 23:20, 21

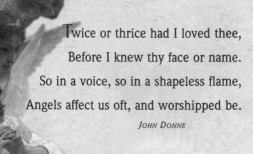

Twice or thrice had I loved thee,

Before I knew thy face or name.

So in a voice, so in a shapeless flame,

Angels affect us oft, and worshipped be.

JOHN DONNE

When one that holds communion
   with the skies
Has fill'd his urn where these
   pure waters rise,
And once more mingles with us
   meaner things,
'Tis e'en as if an angel shook
   his wings.

WILLIAM COWPER

And there was war in heaven. Michael and his angels fought against the dragon, and the dragon and his angels fought back. But he was not strong enough, and they lost their place in heaven.

REVELATION 12:7, 8

Under Angel Eyes

The soul goeth out in the morning,
  Into the world of men:
Into the loving and scorning,
  Into the gossip and gain.

Home she at night returneth
  To prayer and silence and sleep;
Much she hath seen and spurneth,
  Much made her smile and weep.

She beareth the flesh her burden,
  And oft it weigheth her down,

But she thinks of her heavenly
    guerdon,
  The harp and the golden crown.

So down the valley she roameth
  Under her angel's eyes,
Till to the gate she cometh
  The gate of Paradise.

G. S. CAUTLEY

God rules—He rules for us. We may trust Him implicitly. We may venture into the conflict, not rashly, not self-confidently, not presumptuously, but assured that if our strength should fail, there are reserves in heaven, hosts of God, agencies at His command that shall be bidden forth to our rescue.

H. C. McCook

The stars shine on brightly
while Adam and Eve pursue
their way into the far wilderness.
There is a sound through the silence,
as of the falling tears of an angel.

ELIZABETH BARRETT BROWNING

Guardian Angel

With joy the guardian angel sees
A duteous child upon his knees,
And writes in his approving book
Each upward, earnest, holy look.

Light from his pure aerial dream
He springs to meet morn's orient beam,
And pours towards the kindling skies
His clear adoring melodies.

Some glorious seraph, waiting by,
Receives the prayer to waft on high,
And wonders, as he soars, to read
More than we know, and all we need.

JOHN KEBLE

Man is neither angel nor beast;
and the misfortune is that
he who would act the angel
acts the beast.

BLAISE PASCAL

And with the morn
those angel faces smile
Which I have loved long since,
and lost awhile.

JOHN HENRY NEWMAN

Speak ye who best can tell,
ye sons of light,
Angels, for ye behold him,
and with songs
And choral symphonies,
day without night,
Circle his throne rejoicing.

JOHN MILTON

There's not much practical Christianity in the man who lives on better terms with angels and seraphs than with his children, servants, and neighbors.

HENRY WARD BEECHER

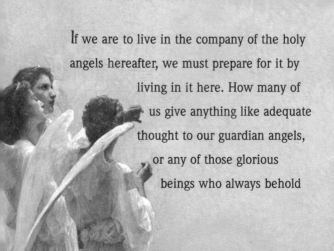

If we are to live in the company of the holy angels hereafter, we must prepare for it by living in it here. How many of us give anything like adequate thought to our guardian angels, or any of those glorious beings who always behold the face of God, and yet cease not

for all our coldness, ingratitude,

to minister tenderly to us! It would

greatly ennoble and elevate us to strive,

in the more conscious company of angels,

to live the angel life.

S.J.C.

All God's Angels

But all God's angels come to us disguised:

Sorrow and sickness, poverty and death,

One after other lift their frowning masks,

And we behold the Seraph's face beneath,

All radiant with the glory and the calm

Of having looked upon the front of God.

JAMES RUSSELL LOWELL

To equip a dull,
respectable person with
wings would be but to
make a parody of an angel.

ROBERT LOUIS STEVENSON

If I have freedom in my love,

And in my soul am free,

Angels alone that soar above

Enjoy such liberty.

RICHARD LOVELACE

...Like an angel,

out of sight,

yet blessing well.

ELIZABETH BARRETT BROWNING

Millions of spiritual creatures
  walk the earth
Unseen, both when we wake,
  and when we sleep:
All these with ceaseless praise
  his works behold
Both day and night.

JOHN MILTON

Angels Unseen

Angels unseen attend the saints,
And bear them in their arms,
To cheer the spirit when it faints,
And guard the life from harms.

The angels' Lord Himself is nigh
To them that love His name;
Ready to save them when they cry,
And put their foes to shame.

JOHN NEWTON

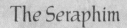

The Seraphim

There are strange ways of serving God;
You sweep a room or turn a sod,
And suddenly, to your surprise,
You hear the whirr of seraphim,
And find you're under God's own eyes
And building palaces for Him.

HERMAN HAGEDORN

If instead of a gem, or even a flower,
we should cast the gift of a loving
thought into the heart of a friend,
that would be giving as the
angels give.

GEORGE MACDONALD

Angels Unawares

In the hours of morn and even,
  In the noon and night,
Trooping down they come from heaven
  In their noiseless flight
To guide, to guard, to warn, to cheer us
  'Mid our joys and cares,
All unseen are hovering near us
  Angels unawares.

When the daylight is declining
   In the western skies,
And the stars in heaven are shining
   As the twilight dies,
Voices on our hearts come stealing
   Like celestial airs,
To our spirit-sense revealing
     Angels unawares.

J. F. WALLER

Keep on loving each other as brothers. Do not forget to entertain strangers, for by so doing some people have entertained angels without knowing it.

HEBREWS 13:1, 2

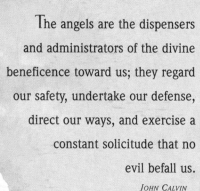

The angels are the dispensers
and administrators of the divine
beneficence toward us; they regard
our safety, undertake our defense,
direct our ways, and exercise a
constant solicitude that no
evil befall us.

JOHN CALVIN

Winged Sentries

Gently he passed;

  the little maiden wept,

Sank down o'erwearied by the dead,

  and slept,

With such a heavenly lustre

  in her face,

You might have fancied angels
  in the place:
Companions through the day
  of our delight
That watch as winged sentries
  all the night.

GERALD MASSEY

Praise the Lord from the heavens,

praise him in the heights above.

Praise him, all his angels,

praise him, all his heavenly hosts.

PSALM 148:1, 2

Harmonious as the voice

of angels singing

before the Eternal Majesty.

SPENSER

Let the Angel Lead

Complain not that the way is long—
　　what road is weary that leads there?
But let the angel take thy hand,
　　and lead thee up the misty stair,
And then with beating heart await
　　the opening of the Golden Gate.

ADELAIDE ANNE PROCTER

We ask for the lifting away of a burden or the averting of a sorrow; our plea is not granted in form, but instead we receive a new impartation of the power of Christ, or an angel from heaven comes to minister to us.

J. R. Miller

May Angels Greet Thee

Angels thy old friends there shall
greet thee,

Glad at their own home now to
meet thee.

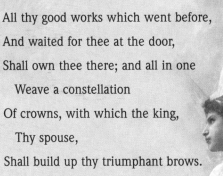

All thy good works which went before,

And waited for thee at the door,

Shall own thee there; and all in one

   Weave a constellation

Of crowns, with which the king,

   Thy spouse,

Shall build up thy triumphant brows.

RICHARD CRAWSHAW

The Lord has sudden unfoldings for souls long closed. For beaten-down stalks He has looks which ripen into a golden harvest; He has warm rains for parched-up grounds; He has royal compassions, at which the hosts of angels break into hallelujahs of praise that ring from heaven to heaven.

COMTESSE DE GASPARIN

1

Like the shields of light
Archangels bear, who, armed with
love and might,
Watch upon heaven's battlements
at night.

ADELAIDE ANNE PROCTER

No More Alone

Yes, one with us in love
  The blessed host above,
And they who wander on a far-off shore;
  One in the great Unseen,
  Though worlds may roll between,
All join the Holy, Holy, Holy to outpour,
    And Christ adore.

O calm and hallow'd hour!
Nor sin nor death hath power,
When that sweet anthem riseth to the
throne;
The angels round us stay,
And evil flees away
Before His face, Who came to leave His own
No more alone.

A. C.

Hope not the cure of sin till
   Self is dead;
Forget it in love's service, and the debt
Thou canst not pay the angels shall forget;
Heaven's gate is shut to him who
   comes alone;
Save thou a soul, and it shall save
   thine own!

JOHN GREENLEAF WHITTIER

Flights of Angels

I can at will, doubt not, as soon as thou,

Command a table in this wilderness,

And call swift flights of angels ministrant

Array'd in glory on my cup to attend.

JOHN MILTON

An angel's is a fine, tender, kind heart. As if we could find a man who had a heart sweet all through, and a gentle will; without subtlety, yet of sound reason; at once wise and simple. He who has seen such a heart, has colours wherewith he may picture to himself what an angel is.

S.J.C.

Angel Psalm

It flooded the crimson twilight
   Like the close of an angel's psalm,
And it lay on my fevered spirit
   With a touch of infinite calm.

It may be that Death's bright angel
   Will speak in that chord again—
It may be that only in heaven
   I shall hear that grand Amen.

ADELAIDE ANNE PROCTER

Holy Friends

O great, befriending natures
　Whom God hath set about
Our human habitations—
　How blank were life, without
Your presences inspiring,
　Your silent, upward call!
Above us, and yet of us,
　One heaven enfolds us all!

ANONYMOUS

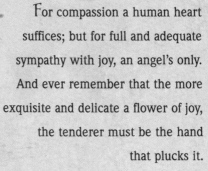

For compassion a human heart
suffices; but for full and adequate
sympathy with joy, an angel's only.
And ever remember that the more
exquisite and delicate a flower of joy,
the tenderer must be the hand
that plucks it.

SAMUEL TAYLOR COLERIDGE

Heaven on Earth

There is more of heaven on earth
  than many dream.
If earth-born senses would permit us see,
And heaven is nearer to this earth I deem,
Than to our holden sight it seems to be.
And there are thoughts of love
  that come and go

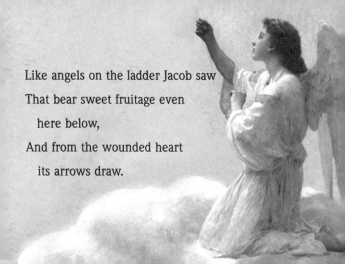

Like angels on the ladder Jacob saw

That bear sweet fruitage even

here below,

And from the wounded heart

its arrows draw.

Touch Our Lips

Here we are, Redeemer, send us!
But because Thy work is fire,
And our lips, unclean and earthly
Breathe no breath of high desire,
Send Thy Seraph from the Altar
Veil'd, but in his bright attire.

Cause him, Lord, to fly full swiftly
   With the mystic coal in hand,
Sin-consuming, soul-transforming
   (Faith and love will understand):
Touch our lips, Thou awful Mercy,
   With thine own keen healing brand.

JOHN KEBLE

Perfect Love

O perfect love that 'dureth long!

Dear growth that shaded by the palms,

And breathed on by the angel's song,

Blooms on in heaven's eternal calms.

JEAN INGELOW

Angelic Love

To love for the sake
of being loved is human,
but to love for the sake
of loving is angelic.

ALPHONSE DE LAMARTINE

Let us not fear to be but a few
among many in our belief. Let us
not fear opposition, suspicion,
reproach, or ridicule.
God sees us, and His
angels, they are
looking on.

They know we are right,

and bear witness to us;

and yet a little while,

and He that cometh shall

come, and will not tarry.

"Now the just shall live by faith."

JOHN HENRY NEWMAN

Breath of Heaven

It is sweet to feel we are
  encircled here,
By breath of angels as the stars
  by heaven;
And the soul's own relations,
  all divine,

As kind as even those of blood;
  and thus,
While friends and kin, like Saturn's
  double rings,
Cheer us along our orbit, we may feel
We are not lone in life, but that earth's part
Of heaven and all things.

P. J. BAILEY

Angels mean messengers
and ministers. Their function
is to execute the plan of divine
providence, even in earthly things.

THOMAS AQUINAS

Hear the Angels Sing

And ye, beneath life's crushing load
Whose forms are bending low,
Who toil along the climbing way
With painful steps and slow;
Look now! for glad and golden hours
Come swiftly on the wing;
Oh! rest beside the weary load,
And hear the angels sing!

E. Hamilton Sears

Hark! the herald angels sing,
"Glory to the newborn King."

CHARLES WESLEY